East Riddlesden

West Yorkshire

THE NATIONAL TRUST

Above The 17th-century plasterwork ceiling in the Dining Room

Right East Riddlesden Hall about 1920; watercolour by E. Riley (Stairhead Chamber)

WOOL AND WEALTH

The story of East Riddlesden Hall has been shaped by the contrasting influences of town and countryside, agriculture and industry, civil war and peace. This intimate 17th-century manor house, built above the River Aire and once the heart of the agricultural estate of Riddlesden, is now a green haven on the edge of urban Keighley.

Your first impression of the place centres on the pond, gently framed by house and trees. It is a simple setting and apparently little changed from early illustrations of the hall. Agriculture was the predominant activity at East Riddlesden Hall. The estate aimed for self-sufficiency, and the massive barns are evidence of a considerable agricultural enterprise.

The wealth to buy the estate and to transform the previous building into a comfortable 17th-century manor house came not only from agriculture, but also from industry. James Murgatroyd, who bought the estate in 1638, had made his fortune in the Halifax woollen cloth industry. After the turbulent years of the English Civil War, and with the fortunes of the Murgatroyd family in decline, the estate eventually passed to a different branch of the family, the Starkies. During the 18th century the estate enjoyed a period of peace and prosperity with the Starkie family. It suffered the uncertainty of absentee landlords throughout the 19th century, when the area was also deeply affected by the Industrial Revolution. The building of the Leeds and Liverpool Canal towards the end of the 18th century cut through the Riddlesden estate. Wool mills, paper mills and even cotton mills sprang up around Keighley, tall chimneys reaching for the sky, and terraced housing spreading along the valleys. East Riddlesden's soot-stained walls still bear witness to Keighley's industrial past.

The Riddlesden estate was gradually sold off during the late 19th and early 20th centuries, and the cottages of Riddlesden village were encroached by 1930s housing and commercial premises. In 1934, under threat of demolition, the hall was purchased by two Keighley brothers, William and John Brigg, who presented it to the National Trust. Today, the scene viewed from the entrance gates of the hall is tranquil and inviting.

Above The soot-stained entrance porch

Left The grain ark of *c.*1600 in the kitchen

BUILDING THE HOUSE

East Riddlesden Hall is primarily a 17th-century house, displaying many of the features typical of a West Yorkshire manor house of the period. However, its building history remains something of a puzzle.

The Medieval Hall

In the early 14th century a hall was built on the site of the now-ruined Starkie wing. Later, a building was constructed to the south of this medieval hall (where the Murgatroyd block now stands). When James Murgatroyd bought the manor and estate of Riddlesden in 1638, the house was very different from what we see today.

The Murgatroyd block

James Murgatroyd had already shown himself to be a keen builder, having built or remodelled several other houses in the Halifax area. During the 1640s he remodelled the south end of East Riddlesden to create the two-storey block we see today. The new building was planned with some style and ostentation. Its most striking features are the two-storey porches at front and back with their distinctive rose windows. The decoration reveals Murgatroyd's quirky sense of style: pinnacles, battlements and a Vitruvian scroll (wave pattern) around the base of this block.

The Starkie wing

Previously, it was assumed that the Starkie wing was a completely new building constructed by Edmund Starkie in the 1690s. It now appears, instead, that Starkie was remodelling the original medieval hall. This theory helps to make sense of the Hall, which lies between the Starkie wing and the Murgatroyd block. The Hall was probably built only as a temporary weather-proof structure, linking Murgatroyd's new block with the original hall, while Murgatroyd carried out his rebuilding programme. Edmund Starkie remodelled the north wing by taking off the roof and wall down to the top of the ground-floor windows. The new upper floor was built in classical style with triangular pediments over the first-floor windows and small external balconies back and front.

Changing spaces

It is apparent throughout the whole house that room divisions and room use were changed over the years, particularly during the 19th century, when various tenant families lived here. Room names today do not match those used in a surviving 1662 inventory. The layout of the Starkie wing is uncertain: all that remains now is the façade. The rest of the wing was demolished by 1905, as it was in very poor condition.

Murgatroyd building	Hall	Starkie wing

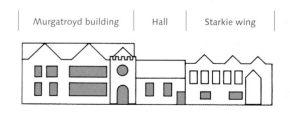

TOUR OF THE HOUSE

The house came to the National Trust with virtually no contents and has been furnished with gifts, bequests, loans and purchases to recreate something of the spirit of the 17th century, but with layers from later times, as in the Green Chamber.

THE HALL

The Hall may appear to be a grand room, but was probably built as a temporary structure that was never completed. Above and to the right of the great fireplace is a recess for another fireplace, which is evidence that James Murgatroyd probably intended to build another floor at this level.

The staircase was installed in 1974 to improve access for visitors: the stairs it replaced were a steep single flight of much cruder construction. The new staircase is of the same period as the house and came from a grammar school in Northamptonshire.

Textiles

Flemish tapestry, c.1600, depicting the story of David and Abigail. The town at the top right is probably Carmel. Wide border of symbolic figures, caryatids (female figures used as pillars), fruit and flowers.

Furniture

Oak side-table, early 17th-century

Armchairs. All are oak 'master's chairs', dating from around 1600–25 and carved with typical Yorkshire designs of the period. Each chair is carved with its own specific pattern on the back panel: vine, key, flower and rose.

Oak benches. Bench with bobbin-turned legs of early 17th-century construction. The other bench dates from the 19th century, but was made up from 17th-century timbers.

Pewter

The selection on the table includes a late 17th- or early 18th-century wine measure, inscribed 'Trinity Hall'; two 18th-century tankards with domed lids and 'S' scroll handles; and a jug of 1832 with massive open spout, scrolled handle and secondary handle below the spout.

Carved stone

Saxon, 8th-century, carved with Celtic knotwork. Lower piece found in 1959, while the drive was being repaired; upper piece found in 1987, while rebuilding a dry-stone wall. The carving perhaps depicts 'The Pelican in her piety, tearing her breast to feed her young'.

Above The ground-floor passage

Right Detail of the decorative border from the Flemish tapestry, c.1600, in the Hall

THE ENTRANCE CHAMBER

This narrow gallery at the head of the stairs is separated from the passage below only by the wide oak floorboards. The good ventilation made it an excellent place for storing grain.

Textiles

The Departure of the Hunt. Copy of a Brussels medieval tapestry in the Louvre. Two early 18th-century embroideries. The early arched panel has finely detailed stitching on the faces and hands of the figures, which were worked professionally before being sold on as a kit for completion by amateur hands. A pair of 19th-century *art needlework pieces*.

Metalwork

17th-century *tin lanterns* have thin sheets of horn incorporated as cheap alternatives to glass.

Spot the difference

Note the difference between embroidery and tapestry: an embroidery is worked by hand with needle and thread; a tapestry is woven and machine-made.

Left The Hall

In 1662 the Red Porch
Chamber was furnished
with one bed with curtains,
one feather bed, one coach
chair and two covered
buffets (stools), leaving very
little room for movement.

Above The Kitchen Chamber

Right The Red Porch
Chamber

Opposite The Stairhead
Chamber

THE KITCHEN CHAMBER

This room and the adjacent Stairhead
Chamber have been substantially altered since
the 17th century. The panelling, ceiling
timbers and ancient floorboards show signs
that room divisions have been changed. The
17th-century panelling is a recurring theme
in the house.

Furniture

Tester bed, 17th-century, Cornish, with carved
headboard. A tester was added to beds as a
status symbol and to protect the sleeper from
dust, insects and any bird droppings from an
open roof space or unplastered ceiling. With
the curtains drawn, a tester bed could offer a
degree of warmth and privacy at a time when

you had to pass through one bedroom to
reach the next.

Textiles

The display of 17th- and 18th-century
embroidery includes a finely worked mid-
17th-century canvas-work pastoral scene
surrounded by figures, with a lion, stag and
leopard. Worked with silk in tent- and cross-
stitch.

Furniture

The *bobbin winder*, 1775–1800, with its hand-
propelled wheel, is a reminder of the local
textile industry.

THE RED PORCH CHAMBER

This small room over the porch would have
been used as a private chamber off the
bedroom. It is now shown as a dressing room.
The large circular window is a typical West
Yorkshire feature, particularly of the Calder
valley, from where James Murgatroyd came.

Furniture

Close stool, oak, *c.*1725. This was designed to
look like a box, when closed; open the lid,
and there is a large white pottery chamber-
pot inside. The close stool gave a greater
degree of comfort than a draughty privy.

Wall mirror, 1675–1700. This 'cushion' mirror
has a walnut veneer frame and its original
silvered plate.

THE STAIRHEAD CHAMBER

The Stairhead Chamber now appears as a large landing, but its shape and use have changed considerably over the years. It is an area that invites speculation by house detectives. The blocked fireplace suggests a different room arrangement at one time: possibly the fireplace end was part of what is now the Kitchen Chamber. The present staircase dates only from the 18th century, and may occupy a different position from the original one.

Pictures

The views of East Riddlesden Hall include a watercolour painted by local artist James H. Betts in 1917. It is believed to have been given to the Bailey family, who were tenants here until 1935. It returned in 2003. The artist appears to have sketched the house before 1905, as the original roofline of the Starkie wing still shows in pencil.

Portraits

Miss Elizabeth Gunter (b.1669), who in 1689 married Nicholas Starkie and lived at East Riddlesden Hall.

Abraham Fothergill (1645–1712). A Keighley lawyer, who practised in London.

Elizabeth Fothergill (1650–1720), wife of Abraham Fothergill. By the time this portrait was painted, Abraham had died, so she is shown in her widow's weeds.

THE GREAT CHAMBER

This is the 'best' chamber, with its high-quality panelling and fireplace and the finest embroideries. The fireplace overmantel is earlier than the panelling with its decorative fruit-wood carving, which would originally have been coloured to match the flowers depicted. During the early 20th century many of the fittings in the house were sold off, and this fireplace was removed to Whinbourne House on the other side of Keighley. When that house was sold, the fireplace was returned here in 1949.

Furniture

Tester bed, with heavily carved tester and headboard. This bed is a composite piece made of various 17th- and 19th-century elements.

Strong-box, 1600–25, used to keep household valuables safe. This heavy, iron-strapped box

Above The brass lantern clock, *c*.1650, made by Thomas Dyde of London, in the Great Chamber

Right The Great Chamber

has a complex locking system with a false keyhole and lock-plate on the front. The real lock is hidden in the centre of the lid, under a stud.

Lantern clock, 1650. Made by Thomas Dyde of London, it has a lion and unicorn ornament on top, only an hour hand, and is weight-driven.

Textiles

Embroidery, 17th-century. Raised-work picture of an allegorical marriage, with animals, buildings and trees; satin embroidered with silk. The picture represents either Charles II and Queen Catherine, or Solomon and the Queen of Sheba.

Embroidery, 1625–50. Raised-work picture of a woman with a castle in the background enclosed by an embroidered oval. Outside the oval are embroidered mythical creatures.

Embroidery, 1650. Raised-work picture of Elijah fed by ravens in a central oval frame, surrounded by animals, trees and buildings.

Embroidery, 17th-century. A pastoral scene in a central oval frame; surrounded by flowering trees, animals and a castle.

THE YELLOW PORCH CHAMBER

This room matches the Red Porch Chamber at other end of the Entrance Chamber (see plan on inside front cover). The rose window, the distinctive architectural feature of both porch rooms, was an expression of the wealth of James Murgatroyd. The panelling and flooring were removed from this room in the early 20th century.

Furniture

Truckle bed, made by the National Trust's furniture conservators in 1984. A truckle or trundle bed was used by servants and was pushed under a tester bed during the day. The ropes strung across the frame could be tightened to give firmer support for the mattress; hence the expression 'sleep tight'.

Above A 17th-century raised-work embroidery of an allegorical marriage. The central figures represent Charles II and Queen Catherine or Solomon and the Queen of Sheba (Great Chamber)

Left Casket, silk on wood, 1660–85, embroidered with various scenes, thought to be based on *The Judgement of Paris*, worked in laid floss silks. The interior has the original pink silk lining with silver trim edges. Inside are an inkwell, sand shaker and several compartments.

The Grey Lady's Chamber is named after the ghost of a Tudor lady of the house, whose husband, returning home unexpectedly, found her with her lover. He starved her to death by imprisoning her in the room, and walled up her lover.

Above The washstand, 1775–1800, in the Green Chamber

Right The Grey Lady's Chamber

Opposite The Green Chamber

THE GREY LADY'S CHAMBER

This is now furnished as the bedroom of the mistress of the house, but in 1662 it was probably the Stairhead Chamber. (The stairs would have come up to the right of the bed as you face it.)

Textiles

Bedspread, cover and pillowcase made in 1961 by Mrs Stanworth, embroidered in blackwork with grape and vine motif. The design is based on a pillow cover in the Victoria & Albert Museum.

A collection of *samplers* worked by young girls in the first half of the 19th century as routine exercises in cross-stitch. They include one worked in 1841 by Agnes Grange with a design of children, flowers, animals and birds

within a floral patterned border. Agnes was born at East Riddlesden Hall on 18 May 1828. Her father was agent and bookkeeper here for the Slingsby family, who were then renting the property.

Furniture

Side-table, 1625–50. A composite piece, the table carcase is from 1625 with various later additions including a new top. It was given by a descendant of the Rishworth family and it is thought that it may originally have been at East Riddlesden Hall. The drawer front was carved later with the initials J R and dated 1713.

Chest, 1500–25 (at foot of bed), continental, with domed lid and frieze carved with trefoils. The front has four Gothic sunken panels with centres carved like church window tracery. This is one of the finest chests in the house.

THE GREEN CHAMBER

This room has a different character to the rest of the house, as the painted panelling is 18th-century, and some of the furniture is made from mahogany, which was imported from the 1720s. The window was blocked up in the late 17th century, when a new chimneystack was added to service a fireplace in the Dining Room below.

THE DRAWING ROOM

The importance of this room is shown by the decorative plaster ceiling and the chimneypiece, which date from James Murgatroyd's rebuilding of the house in the 1640s.

The plasterwork is similar to the work of Francis Lee, who inherited some of the moulds of the celebrated Wakefield school, which flourished in the late 16th century. However, Lee died in 1638, so he cannot have been directly responsible for the ceiling in this room. It is more likely to be the work of the colleagues to whom he bequeathed his tools and moulds, Luke Dobson and John Maude.

The *fireplace*, with inlaid panels and heavily carved work, seems old-fashioned for the inscribed date of 1648. The inscription is believed to be from Psalm 144, which praises daughters as the cornerstones ('coihn') of the family.

Furniture

Oak settle, 1625–50, eight recessed panels in back. This settle matches the fireplace in the use of inlaid wood; ebony and boxwood, in floral and geometric designs.

Chest on stand, 1700–25, walnut. The stand is contemporary with the chest but was not made for it.

Glazed cupboard on chest, 18th-century. These two chests represent a development in form, raising a chest or cupboard on top of a stand or chest.

Four-leaf screen, 1683, made up of a massive engraved map of the biblical land of Canaan and a topographical view of the city of Jerusalem. The map was made by John More, who was born in Yorkshire and died in 1592, and published by Robert Green.

Daybed, 1660–75, walnut, with cane back panel and seat, and eight turned legs with scrolled feet. The decorative scrolling was a new fashion in the second half of the 17th century. The use of walnut and cane was the height of fashion in the late 17th century. In marked contrast to the earlier oak furniture in the house, this piece shows the new sophistication of furniture after the Restoration in 1660.

Ceramics

Leeds creamware (in glazed cupboard on chest). Creamware is a term given to a fine pottery with a yellow glaze, varying from a deep buttery yellow to a milky white. The Leeds pottery was the most important manufacturer of creamware in the 18th century after Josiah Wedgwood in Staffordshire. Leeds pottery is most famous for its pierced creamware.

Above The Drawing Room fireplace

Opposite The Drawing Room

Left 18th-century Leeds creamware in the Drawing Room

THE DINING ROOM

This room was called 'His Own Parlour' in the 1662 Inventory, when John Murgatroyd probably used it as both his bedroom and private office.

As in the Drawing Room, the plasterwork ceiling dates from the 1640s and was probably done by itinerant members of the West Yorkshire school of plasterers. The moulds were probably made 50 years before.

Furniture

Oak cupboard, 1600, three-tier buffet. Originally a two-tier cupboard with a later top section, with fluted frieze, used for display. It was once at Ponden Hall, and was given to the National Trust in 1946 by Mr H. Brigg of Kildwick Hall. This 'vast oak dresser' is said to have been the cupboard described in the opening pages of Emily Brontë's *Wuthering Heights*.

Textiles

Early 20th-century Persian Heriz *carpet* with medallion design. It is placed on the table in the fashion of the 17th century, when carpets were considered too valuable to walk on.

THE KITCHEN

In December 1996 the floorboards of the room above, the Kitchen Chamber, were taken up and relaid. During this process it was noted that the Kitchen ceiling was intended originally to be open woodwork, not plastered: the beams are planed and have chamfered edges. It is also possible that the Kitchen was once a panelled room, as there appeared to be wooden plugs in the walls for attaching panels.

Picture

The Airedale Heifer, coloured lithograph, *c*.1830. This prize-winning beast lived at East Riddlesden. She was slaughtered in 1830 after being severely injured and was found to weigh 188 stone 8 lbs and to have a girth of 11ft 11in.

Furniture

The most notable piece of furniture here is the *grain ark* of *c*.1600. This massive oak chest, used for storing grain, is the only piece of furniture that came to the National Trust in 1934 with the property. It may be one of the arks recorded in the 1662 Inventory.

Above The copper curfew, 1575–1626 (from the French *'couvre feu'*: 'cover fire'), is a rare survival. It served as an overnight fireguard and kept the embers smouldering to make relighting an easier task in the morning

Opposite The Kitchen

Right The Dining Room

THE OUTBUILDINGS

THE BOTHY

The battlemented building to the left of the main entrance to the house is known as the Bothy, and is now the reception centre. A bothy was a building used to house farm workers. The room which is now the shop has traces of a plasterwork freize, indicating that it was for a person of more importance than a farm worker or servant. This may indicate that the room was for James Murgatroyd's own use, while work was being done on the main block. Later, this room may have been used by the estate steward, and the rest of the building for servant and farm workers accommodation.

Outside, the lintels over the doors are characteristic of the crude carving which is such a feature of the hall. Over one door the initials JMM stand for James and Mary Murgatroyd, and JSM for John and Susan Murgatroyd. Above are two reliefs depicting King Charles I and Queen Henrietta Maria with the motto 'Vive le roy' ('Long live the king'). As this was dated 1643, a year after the outbreak of the Civil War, it was a brave declaration of loyalty on the part of James Murgatroyd.

THE BARNS

The Great Barn has undergone few changes since the 17th century and is one of the finest barns in the north of England. It measures 37 metres long by 12 metres wide. The barn retains many of its original features including the flagged threshing floors running between the two sets of great arched portals, the beaten earth and cobble main floor, some of the stalls, and the glorious riven oak roof structure. The blind recesses in the walls were probably used for resting lanterns. The barn would have housed cattle over the winter and provided storage for their fodder. The barn today houses a collection of agricultural equipment including ploughs, a chaff-cutter, a winnowing-machine and a selection of carts.

The Airedale Barn measures 27 metres long by 12 metres wide. The original great aisle posts were removed in the Second World War to create more storage space for the Ministry of Food. In the early 1990s the National Trust restored this barn, putting back the great aisle posts. The barn is now available for community use.

Left The Great Barn

Opposite The interior of the Great Barn in the early 20th century

TOUR OF THE GARDEN

THE GROUNDS

At the front of the house the grounds are simple and understated, providing a contrast with the more formal gardens at the back. It is a tranquil scene set around the pond with its resident ducks. Ivy is encouraged to ramble over the Starkie wing. Plants are predominantly native. Mature beech and wild cherry trees enclose the grounds and create a feeling of intimacy. The lane leads down to the lower field where a grass maze invites young and old for a circular ramble.

THE FORMAL GARDEN

On leaving the house by the back porch, a short avenue of apple and pear trees draws your eye into the garden. This small formal garden was created by the National Trust in 1972 to a design by Graham Stuart Thomas. The garden is intimate and enclosed, but with glimpses of the hills on the other side of the Aire river valley. An evergreen *Ilex* x *altaclerensis* 'Hodginsii' hedge planted around the south-east corner of the garden helps to keep it sheltered. Through the gap at the end of the hedge, the plant sales area, where all the plants are peat-free, offers an unbroken view of the valley.

The character of the garden is defined by formal elements such as lawns, dwarf hedges and the miniature 'avenue' of pyramidal-pruned apple and pear trees. Mixed flower borders are designed for subtle plant associations and for continuity of colour and interest throughout the year. The irregular shape of the area is disguised by the arrangement of the borders. The walls are covered with species of climbing plants: roses, quince, clematis, and ivy. In early summer philadelphus and honeysuckle fill the garden with their scent.

The sunken rose garden is planted with *Rosa* 'Dusky Maiden' interspersed with *Cyclamen hederifolium*, which flowers in early autumn. *Robinia pseudoacacia* 'Umbraculifera' are planted on one lawn, and make a chequered pattern of shade. They are pruned hard every two years to create a spherical shape. The ruined façade of the Starkie wing, covered in a tangle of clematis, gives a romantic backdrop to the garden, and the border in front spills over with perennials and roses.

Follow the scented lavender border to the left of the back porch and around the corner of the house to find the Herb Border.

Opposite The planting at the front of the house is kept simple and understated

Below The Starkie wing

THE HERB BORDER

This is situated in a sunny position at the top of a steep slope overlooking the grass maze. In the 17th century herbs would have been in daily use at East Riddlesden Hall. Not only were they used for cooking and medicine but also for insect repellent, dyes for cloth, disinfectant and furniture polish. The herb border follows themes from Culpeper's *Herbal* (1653). You can admire these unassuming plants with their soft and subtle colours, muse over their intriguing history and enjoy their perfume.

Lavender (*Lavandula* species)
This highly scented herb would have been strewn around the floors to act as an insect repellent, and was also scattered between bed linen to add a fresh clean scent.

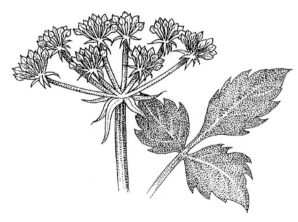

Right Lovage

Opposite Lavender in the Herb Border

Tansy (*Tanacetum vulgare*)
The delicate fern-like leaf and small dense mustard-coloured flowers make this an attractive herb. It was popularly used as a disinfectant. At Easter it was made into 'Tansy', a rich custardy pudding.

Marjoram (*Origanum* species)
Marjoram was used by ladies to put in bags and to sweeten washing water. Its leaves were rubbed over heavy oak furniture and floors to give a fragrant polish. It was also placed in pails of fresh milk to stop it from going sour.

Marsh Mallow (*Althaea officinalis*)
Pretty pink and white blooms appear in late summer. This is the original source of the confectionary of this name. Its powdered root thickens in water and it was heated with sugar to create a soothing, sweet paste.

Lovage (*Levisticum officinale*)
A handsome herb which can be used in a variety of different ways, from laying the leaves in shoes to revive weariness, to a tasty addition to stock, stews, cheese and salads.

Rosemary (*Rosmarinus officinalis*)
Resinous rosemary would have been burnt in sick chambers to purify the air. During the plague it was carried by travellers in order to help ward off disease.

From the Herb Border, retrace your steps, and at the far end of the Formal Garden, wander through the gate in the wall to discover a place of peace and tranquillity.

PRODUCE IN THE GARDEN

The garden boasts many plants and trees with edible fruit. The Falcon Mews contains a large fig tree, a quince and a plum tree. Bushes of blackcurrants, redcurrants and whitecurrants face the Culpeper border. Pear and apple trees climb the walls of the house, and line the avenue in the Formal Garden. A morello cherry is fan-trained and clings to the north-facing house wall in the sunken rose garden.

Robinson believed that the garden should become a place dedicated to the honourable pleasures of rejoicing the eye, refreshing the nose and renewing the spirit.

Above The late Victorian garden writer William Robinson, who pioneered the style of informal planting seen in the Wild Garden

Opposite Aquilegia in the Wild Garden

THE WILD GARDEN

The Wild Garden, opened in 2000, was designed to contrast with the Formal Garden, combining a collection of local apple varieties with 'wild garden' planting based on the theories of William Robinson. This new garden reflects the passing seasons, providing interest from spring through to late summer, and also offers habitat for a variety of wildlife.

William Robinson was an influential late Victorian garden writer. He detested Victorian formal schemes with plants in neat rows, and found the bright colours of annual bedding schemes abominable. Essentially, Robinson's wild gardening was the placing of hardy exotic plants (known as herbaceous perennials today) under conditions where they would thrive without further care. He loved his plants to naturalise in grasses and follow as closely as possible the type of plant groups you would see in the wild, creating great swathes of colour.

Here in the Wild Garden the design is kept simple, creating a feeling of enclosure with sweeping curves and broad groups of plants. Herbaceous perennials have been naturalised in grass. The glade in the centre is surrounded by taller grasses, whilst bulbs, perennials and wildflowers are planted amongst the grasses for flowering in early spring through to late summer. Geraniums, foxgloves, crocosmia and hemerocallis blend with grasses and wildflowers such as Columbines, Meadow Cranesbill, Herb Robert, Betony and Campion to create a changing carpet of colour. At the rear of the garden the boundary planting becomes thicker, and carpets of bluebells and wood anemone produce a woodland feel.

True wild gardening is gardening as nature would have it: no confines, pretence or inhibitions; plants allowed to naturalise and self seed. The massed profusion gives the feeling of a living tapestry.

Seasons of colour in the Wild Garden

The garden comes to life in *spring*; there are fresh cool greens, and sweeps of pale daffodils, blue violets, cowslips and fragrant white narcissi.

In *May* a vibrant sea of blue camassias crowds the grasses. Pale blue aquilegia, campanula and foxgloves blend to form a pastel palette

By *late summer and into early autumn,* scarlet berries appear on the rowan trees. Deep oranges, russets and scarlet create a mellow mood. Tawny-coloured day lilies, deep orange daisies and scarlet *Crocosmia* 'Lucifer' punctuate the edges of the glade. The season draws to a close, and cyclamen give their final show of pinks and whites.

TIMELINE

7th century	Site cleared and settled by an Angle named Hrethel
c.1086–1124	Gospatric and his descendants hold the site
12th–14th century	De Montalt family possess the estate
Early 14th century	A hall was constructed where the remains of the Starkie wing now stand
c.1402	Elizabeth de Montalt married Robert Paslew
c.1402–1571	Paslew family hold the estate
c.1402	West Riddlesden Hall built; tenanted by the Maude family who paid rent to East Riddlesden
1571	Robert Rishworth, son-in-law of Walter Paslew, leases the Riddlesden estate
1602	Robert Rishworth leaves East Riddlesden Hall and half the estate to his son John, and West Riddlesden Hall and the other half of the estate to his wife Ellen
1638	James Murgatroyd buys the manor and estate of East Riddlesden
1640s	James Murgatroyd carries out building works on the house and bothy
1653	Death of James Murgatroyd
1672	East Riddlesden Hall in part-ownership of the Murgatroyds and Edmund Starkie, with Edmund Starkie in residence
1690s	Edmund Starkie remodels the west wing
1708	Edmund Starkie obtains full possession
Early 19th century	Elizabeth and Catherine Starkie marry into the Bence and Bacon families, and their property therefore passes to their husbands. They live in Suffolk and are absentee landlords

Above Detail of a 17th-century Flemish tapestry in the Entrance Chamber

Opposite Detail of a carved serpent on the back of a Lancashire oak chair in the Kitchen Chamber

19th century	Various family groups are tenants at East Riddlesden Hall, living in one or two rooms each. Various tenant farmers on the estate
By 1891	Bailey family appear to be in control of the bulk of the estate
By 1905	Starkie wing dismantled except for façade, and remaining house in very poor condition
c.1860s–1930s	Estate sold off piecemeal by the Bacon and Bence families
1934	William and John Brigg of Keighley purchase East Riddlesden Hall and present it to the National Trust

WEALTH AND CONFLICT

England in the 17th century was a place of conflict and change. Events at East Riddlesden Hall at that time were no different. The purchase of the East Riddlesden estate and the rebuilding of the manor reflected the wealth of one man, James Murgatroyd. Perhaps surprisingly, he began his rebuilding programme in the same year, 1642, that the English Civil War began to tear the country apart.

Top The 17th-century plasterwork frieze in the Dining Room

Above The royalist James Murgatroyd commissioned the crudely carved heads of Charles I and Queen Henrietta Maria that decorate the castellated Bothy

Opposite Elizabeth Gunter married Nicholas Starkie and lived at East Riddlesden in the early 18th century

James Murgatroyd came from the Calder valley near Halifax, where he was a rich wool merchant and entrepreneur. At the time that he purchased the East Riddlesden estate in the Aire valley, the wool industry in the area was expanding into a large cottage industry using water from the local streams.

Murgatroyd was a man of strong character and idiosyncratic taste. Charles I twice offered him a knighthood, which he refused, preferring to pay fines rather than accept such an expensive honour. James Murgatroyd's control of his family was patriarchal. He reconstructed the family seat at Warley and either built or remodelled at least three houses for his children. East Riddlesden was selected for his son John.

When James Murgatroyd purchased East Riddlesden from John and Richard Rishworth in 1638, part of the purchase agreement was that the Rishworths retained rooms at the manor for their own use. This probably meant that they occupied the old medieval hall. If so, it could partly explain why James Murgataroyd only rebuilt the southern block of the house. However, the Civil War affected many aspects of everyday life, including business. James Murgatroyd was a staunch

Royalist in an area of Parliamentarian sympathy. If, as seems likely, James's business dealings were adversely affected by the war, this provides another strong reason to explain why building was carried no further.

James Murgatroyd died in 1653. His sons do not appear to have inherited his entrepreneurial abilities and, without his influence, things began to go wrong at East Riddlesden. When John Murgatroyd died in 1662, an inventory was taken, showing the value of the goods and chattels at East Riddlesden Hall. Unfortunately, however, he left no will, with the result that his sons, James and John, disputed ownership of the manor and estate. John apparently mortgaged East Riddlesden to Edmund Starkie without his brother's knowledge. Edmund was the son of Nicholas Starkie of Huntroyd near Burnley, whom Grace Murgatroyd had married in 1635. It took a court case to settle the matter.

By 1672 East Riddlesden Hall was in part-ownership of the Murgatroyds and Edmund Starkie. We know that Edmund Starkie was in residence then, as the hearth tax returns for that year name him. During the 1690s Starkie remodelled the north wing, so by that time he must have felt confident of his tenure.

STABILITY AND PROGRESS

LEEDS TO LIVERPOOL CANAL

The Leeds to Liverpool Canal greatly improved transport across the Pennines, and made Keighley an important town in the Aire Gap. The Bingley to Skipton section of the canal, opened in 1773, cut right through the East Riddlesden estate. Today, cross over the road at the main entrance to find the canal and walk along the towpath.

Edmund Starkie finally obtained full possession of the East Riddlesden estate in 1708. By that time the house was at its fullest extent following his remodelling of the north wing in the 1690s. East Riddlesden settled down to a century of stability with the Starkie family. England, too, enjoyed a period of comparative domestic stability throughout the 18th century: the revolutions that occurred were agricultural and industrial.

Edmund Starkie, however, did not have long to enjoy full possession of the estate, for he died in 1712, and his nephew Nicholas took over control. Nicholas married Elizabeth Gunter and it is probably her portrait that now hangs in the Stairhead Chamber. East Riddlesden passed through several generations of the Starkie family. Nicholas was followed as head of the family by his son, Edmund Starkie of Preston, who placed his brother Nicholas at East Riddlesden as his agent.

Throughout the 18th century East Riddlesden enjoyed the status of a gentlemen's secondary residence. Most of the Starkies were farmers, and the massive barns and water mill on the Rive Aire served a substantial agricultural enterprise. Evidence of agricultural activity on the estate appears in a lease agreement of 1760: 'Mr Edmund Starkie has taken all Slate of the West or Great Barn and Slated it anew: He has likewise removed the Old Mill and Kiln to where the New Mill Stands on the River Ayre…'

In 1797 the last male Starkie of Riddlesden, Nicholas, died, leaving a widow and daughters. The scene was set for more change at East Riddlesden Hall.

Absentee landlord and tenant farmers

During the 1820s East Riddlesden enjoyed the reflected glory of the celebrated Airedale Heifer, fattened on the estate. But it was decline that was to be the decisive characteristic of East Riddlesden Hall in the 19th century. When the last Nicholas Starkie's daughters married, their property, by law, passed to their husbands. Both girls married men of property in Suffolk and went to live there. From then on, the East Riddlesden estate suffered because it had absentee landlords. A succession of tenant farmers occupied the estate throughout the 19th century and the early part of the 20th century. The farm tenants were taken from three main families, the Denbys, the Horners and the Baileys. From the second half of the century, small parts of the estate began to be sold off. The house received no more architectural improvements, and its condition deteriorated. It was subdivided, and had as many as four families living in it.

Yet East Riddlesden Hall was still a very important part of the local community, and provided the venue for Queen Victoria's Golden Jubilee in 1887.

Above The Starkie wing in 1904

Opposite East Riddlesden Hall in the early 19th century

Far-reaching changes
occurring in the textile
industry, such as the
introduction of machinery
and a move from cottage
industry to factory system,
heralded the start of the
growth of Keighley as an
industrial town. The first
cotton mill started
production in 1780, and by
1805 there were ten mills in
the Keighley area. The first
worsted mills arrived here
around 1808, and by the
1850s there were about 30.

Above The prize-winning
Airedale Heifer was bred at
East Riddlesden. The house
appears in the background
of this colour lithograph

AN END AND A BEGINNING

At the beginning of the 20th century East Riddlesden Hall was in a poor state, and the break up of the estate continued. The Starkie wing was almost entirely demolished in 1905. Eight years later, a large part of the interior fittings of the house – fireplaces, panelling, plaster ceilings and doors – was sold. Rumours were rife that the house was to be pulled down. In 1913 William A. Brigg, then the Mayor of Keighley, and his twin brother John J. Brigg, repurchased most of the fittings in the hope that a public fund could be raised to secure the house's permanent preservation. This attempt failed, and in 1921 the estate was offered for sale by auction, but no acceptable bids were received.

Below Despite the encroachment of Keighley, East Riddlesden today retains much of its rural setting

In 1933 what remained of the East Riddlesden estate was sold to a builder who intended to develop it. But the builder was prepared to consider an offer for the hall and the immediately surrounding area so that they could be retained for posterity. The Brigg brothers stepped in again and were able to purchase it. On 31 May 1934 they presented the deeds of East Riddlesden to the National Trust, thus ensuring the property's survival.

Throughout these troubled times, and on into a new life with the National Trust, the house and grounds remained an important focal point for the local community. There was boating, fishing and skating on the pond. Sometimes, when the river flooded onto the lower fields and then froze, that too was used for skating. There were parties in the Barn, and meetings in the Bothy. The Silver Jubilee of King George V in 1935 was celebrated with a party in the Airedale Barn, and from 1941 until 1982 the Riddlesden Brotherhood and Veterans Association met regularly in the ground floor of the Bothy. During the Second World War the Airedale Barn was used for food storage by the Ministry of Food. Cricket was, and still is, played on the lower fields.

It may be difficult today, with East Riddlesden Hall surrounded by 20th-century housing and commercial enterprises, to imagine the predominance of farming in this area. But it remains a small and peaceful remnant of green countryside amid the surrounding urban landscape.